Academy on High 1
Mary the Hebrew

Belle Twigg

Academy on High 1

Copyright 2015, 2019 by Belle Twigg. All Rights Reserved.

All rights reserved. No part of this book may be reproduced in any form or by any electronic or mechanical means including information storage and retrieval systems, without permission in writing from the author. The only exception is by a reviewer, who may quote short excerpts in a review.

Belle Twigg

Printed in the United States of America

Fellowship of Mystery

www.fellowshipofmystery.com

ISBN-13: 9781090939944

We would love to hear how this book has assisted you in your journey. Please leave a comment or review of this book.

Contents

- Preface 5
- Introduction 6
- Christ and Kadmon 12
- A Story 17
  - Birthing 20
  - Growth 21
  - Naming 23
  - Questioning 24
  - Nearness 27
  - Mary 29
  - Secret 31
- Space of Creation 32
- Sons of God 41
- Maturing Sons 44
- Experiential Knowing 46
- God 49
- Concealing and Revealing 50
- Relationship 58
- Third Point 60
- Model 63
- Movement 66
- Index 67
  - Recommended Books 68
  - About the Author 69

PREFACE

In this study, we'll be looking at a systems model for understanding the orderly way that God has structured the worlds. By "worlds", I'm not only speaking about the planets. We exist on many different levels. There is a physical level we can interact with by way of our body. We have emotional, intellectual, imaginal and spiritual worlds, all of which are held within us.

We are constantly moving through and within different levels (or states) of consciousness. All these worlds and states of awareness are experienced within us. Even the physical world is interacted with and known within our own being.

Through Christ, all these worlds, dimensions and being have been created. Each of these is spirit and living because he is spirit and life.

The multidimensional model referred to as the Tree of Life may help us understand who we are and all that is held within us. Jesus the Christ (who is the Tree of Life) exemplifies how we can grow as Sons of God. The Tree serves as a kind of map and compass we may use to develop and nurture our relationship with God, others, ourselves and his dominion.

In the beginning volumes of Academy on High, many new concepts are introduced without fully explaining them. Do not worry about trying to fully understand what each word or concept means. As the study progresses, you will develop an intuitive feel for them.

INTRODUCTION

This is an examination of ancient Hebraic spiritual science, viewed from a Christ-centered perspective. As we go through this study, we'll be exploring some of what may be called, "universals". In other words, while this is Hebraic and written for Christian mystics, much of the content may be found within other spiritual traditions as well.

In the Hebrew tradition, spiritual science has historically been explored and expounded upon using what is called the Tree of Life. As Christians, we identify that Tree as corresponding to Christ, who is the last Adam. The Jews, who (in general) do not acknowledge the individual named Jesus as the Messiah, do associate the Tree of Life with Adam. Specifically, the Tree of Life is connected to the primordial, or first, Adam who holds within himself all expressions of Adam and creation as we know it.

Philo of Alexandria referred to this first Adam as, "the Heavenly Man, who has no participation in corruption, has no physical essence, but is the image of God and is neither male nor female, being an incorporeal intelligence".

The Midrash speaks of the first Adam when it says, "Thou hast formed me behind and before, meaning before the first and after the last day of creation. It is written in Scripture that the Spirit of God moved upon the face of the waters, meaning, the spirit of Adam, the Messiah."

Rabbi Akiva points our attention toward the idea that man was made in the image of a God-created pattern. There is an archetype, who is the first Adam, the heavenly man who is also called, mystically, the son of man. In this way, Akiva infers that this Adam, who is the first and last, is the image and likeness of God. This Adam is the fullness of all who are Adam and holds within himself all that exists.

> Where there is neither Greek nor Jew, circumcision nor uncircumcision, Barbarian, Scythian, bond nor free: but Christ is all, and in all. (Col 3:11)

In the *Zohar*, this primordial Adam is referred to as, "the high man" and the "heavenly man".

The Logos, the Word (who is the original image of God), is the heavenly embodiment of the emanated thought of God. It is this original image who created physical man. The heavenly man, primordial Adam, created the earthly man, who is also called Adam. In this way, man is an image of his Creator, who is the first and last Adam, the heavenly man, the Son of God, the Word.

When we speak (in spiritual science) of the Holy Temple, the vessel, the house of creation or the Tree of Life as a model, we are (at the highest level of meaning) referring to the first Adam who we, as believers in Jesus, call Christ. But those terms also rightly refer to us as individuals and as the corporate body of Christ, because we are in him and exist as his image. We have been created by Christ of his own essence.

> yet for us there is but one God, the Father, from whom are all things and we exist for Him; and one Lord, Jesus Christ, by whom are all things, and we exist through Him. (I Cor. 8:6)

This first Adam (primordial Adam) is sometimes called Adam Kadmon. Adam Kadmon has also been described as the original, collective soul from which all men are descended. In other words, as an archetype Adam Kadmon is representative of that which is precreation, (prior to any creation) and holds within himself all of creation. Therefore, whenever you read herein the name, "Adam Kadmon," I am directing your attention toward Christ.

> For by him were all things created, that are in heaven, and that are in earth, visible and invisible, whether *they be* thrones, or dominions, or principalities, or powers: all things were created by him, and for him: And he is before all things, and by him all things consist (Col. 1:16-17)

"Rabbi, the Word was concealed with the blessed Holy One. He revealed it in the Academy on High. Here it is: When the Concealed of all Concealed verged on being revealed, it produced at first a single point, which ascended to become thought. Within, it drew all drawings, engraved all engravings, carving within the Concealed Holy Lamp a graving of one hidden design, Holy of Holies, a deep structure emerging …." (Maria the Hebrew)

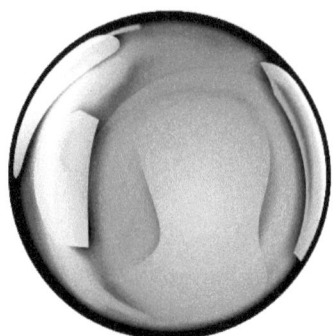

A point has position but no magnitude. It has no measure. It is beyond measure. A point is no thing but it is everything and within everything. It is all that exists. All that exists is held within he who is existence itself. He is the point that contains and sustains all points. He is eternal.

Allah *(the Being Who exists necessarily, by himself, comprising all the attributes of perfection, see: Lane's Arabic-English Lexicon)* **is the light of the heavens and the earth** *(see: Col 1:17). (As a name, Allah signifies timeless existence, the source of all that exists)*

The similitude *(likeness, a metaphor/ it is not properly expressed with words, equal to himself as the will and thought of God. This is the expansion of himself as the Voice/Word)* **of his light** *(Word)* **is that of a niche** *(point/hollow place)*, **within which is a lamp** *(all potential-- the voice, will, knowledge, understanding and wisdom of the Word).*

The lamp is within a glass *(plasmatic, translucent)* **orb** *(space of creating/sphere of being).*

The glass, as it were, is a shining star *(the Son/ Stars of Influence – the true being of the sons is as a shining star whose being is the Light. They are the light of, in, through, by and for the Light)* (Surah, Qur'an)

*Parentheses are commentary upon the original text.

CHRIST AND KADMON

Picture a sphere. For the sake of illustration, we'll call this sphere, Adam Kadmon.

Nothing in the universe exists for man until man has his first thought of it. If a man can think it, it is possible.

Inside of this sphere, envision another sphere. We'll call this sphere, Adam ha Rishon. So, we have a sphere inside of a sphere. One sphere existing within another sphere. But the first sphere is prior to creation. It is uncreated. That which is inside of the first sphere (the smaller sphere) was created.

Unity, One, Consciousness

Similarly, we could say that Adam ha Rishon exists within Adam Kadmon. If we were to try to simplify this, we could say there is an earthly image of the heavenly man. (A sphere within a sphere.)

The Adam of the garden narrative holds within himself the entire human race. But, the Adam of the garden is held within the primordial Adam, whom Christians call Christ.

In this symbolic illustration, there is Adam Kadmon who holds Adam ha Rishon. Adam ha Rishon holds within himself humanity.

Adam Kadmon, sometimes called the primordial man, refers to the one who holds all of humanity within himself. But he also holds all beings, all spirits, all creation and all potential for creation.

Christ is as the thought, action and voice of God. He is the original vessel of creation. As such, Christ is the point in the center that is referred to as the foundation stone (or the central pillar). He is also the sphere of creation and all that is held within creation. He is the sustainer of all creation. Christ is the Creator.

Let me say this again. Christ is the thought, action and voice of God. He is the vessel of creation. Christ is the uncreated sphere who holds within himself all that might ever fill the space. Christ is also the point in the center of creation, which determines the form of creation, its location and position. This center point is referred to as the foundation stone, or the central pillar.

Christ is everything that is held within the space of creation. He is the sustainer of all creation, and he is the Creator. Christ is the Word, the namer of creation.

A STORY

Mary floated in a sphere of water. As a golden droplet, she danced in the rippling water of the womb. Her mother's womb was like a universe concealed within itself, nurturing Mary's frame.

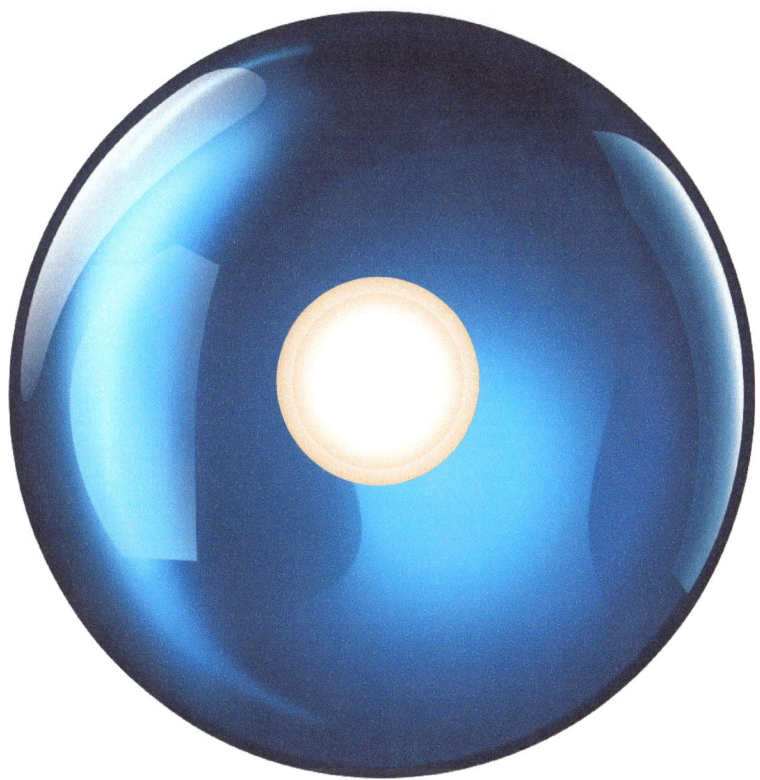

The king looked upon his image from above. There, as if within a woman's womb, a child was forming. Nurtured inside a living universe, the child concealed within herself worlds, even though she was a child not yet birthed. The child, like her mother, held within her a myriad of reflections of consciousness. These were like fractalizations. Wombs inside of wombs were all held inside the house of creation. Eve within Eve, within Eve, like a woven basket of light and contrast, radiating from numinous to denseness and returning around to its first point of creation. Vessels inside of vessels, each an arena of experience. Each vessel was a temple created by, in, and holding Divinity.

BIRTHING

Mary felt the pressure pushing and pulling on her as though she were a lump of clay, waiting to know her form. She felt the cool sting of dryness and separation. Breath rushed into her small frame even as the face of the king pulled back, concealing himself yet further from Mary.

GROWTH

Much of Mary's early life was blurred like a faded, distant, dream; dreams in the watch of the night. As Mary grew older, shadowy memories, shapes, sounds and impressions touched her. In her dreams she envisioned her life before she was born, when she dwelled in the above. Come morning's light, the dreams were reworked into a construct acceptable and fitting to the realm of action. This was Mary's reality. She was a physical being whose feet and hands shaped the world as they touched physicality, not a spiritual being of her dreams.

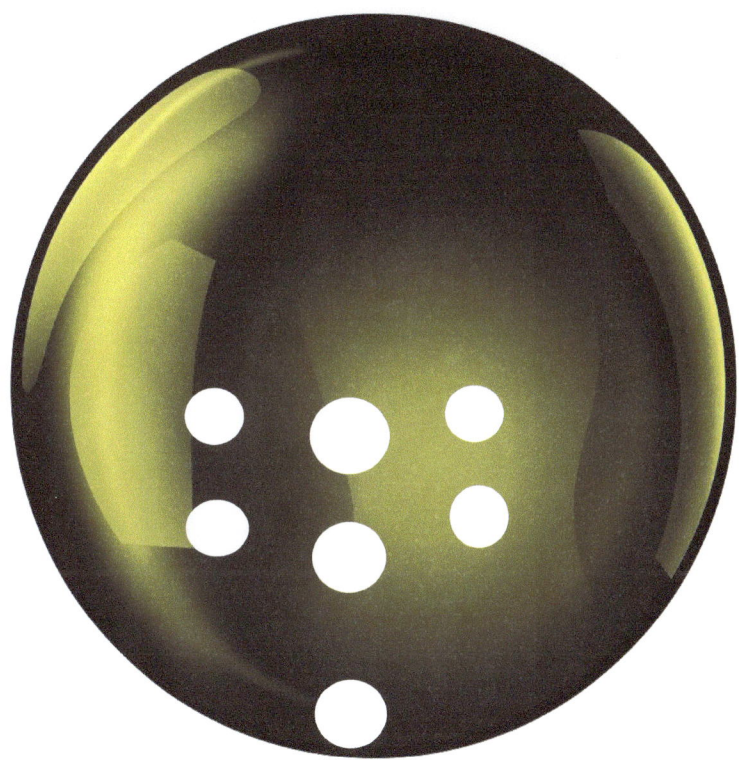

Her breathing was a moving breath. Living breath reached out and touched all that was within her. Just as wind moves the leaves of a tree, Mary's breath moved. Her sound, voice and speech resonated through and beyond the air, touched the atmosphere, stretched into the imaginal, and named her sense of creation. All that was within her, was herself. But somehow, she was more than the sum of it all.

NAMING

She sensed that her name wasn't really Mary. The king had ensured that in preparation for stepping into her true name, even as a child, she was trained and pointed toward her high calling. This made it easier for her to remember bits and pieces, glimpses of who she had once been. Now and again, she would see a flash, as a glimmer of lightning passing just moments before, revealing messages from the realm of light and knowledge of her king, who sustains all within himself.

QUESTIONING

One Sabbath evening, the king sat Mary down for a serious talk. "Child, do you know who you are? Do you know who formed you? Do you know of what you are formed? To where you will return? Who are you, child?" With this, the king left her, giving her time to think about his questions.

But no answer that Mary came up with seemed right. She was not this body, her experiences or her name. Mary went to bed night after night, month after month with no answer to the king's questions. She wondered if, perhaps, it was a trick. Maybe, there were no answers at all.

One day, Mary sat at a streams edge, drawing in the mud with her small finger as children sometimes do. She pushed the tip of one finger into the clay. Upon removing it, light danced on its moist surface causing the mundane to shimmer like precious stone. Mary gazed deeply into the shimmering reflection, finding within it a vision of her face, as though the clay had been fashioned as an indistinct mirror. Deeper and deeper she was drawn into the reflection, falling within herself, moving as through tunnels of a starry night.

The sounds of the babbling water beside her, the wind rustling the meadow flowers and bee's wings touching the air … disappeared. Silence reigned here in the wilderness within her, as she was carried from world to world.

But soon she heard trumpets, drums, a choir of one voice, a symphony of harmony. The music of the spheres seemed to call to her and simultaneously praise the king. There was infinite rejoicing with all sound, no sound and pure essence of being.

Her movement stopped. It was as though all the stars of influence stood waiting, watching, full of wonder. And then he appeared to her.

NEARNESS

When she returned to her normal state of awareness, she looked at the gold of the clay. She said, "I am that". She looked up into the light of the sun. She said, "I am that". She looked at the flowing water of the stream. She said, "I am that. I am all of this and more. But I am none of this at all".

She closed her eyes and rested in her king's presence. She knew the answer to the king's question. She said, "It is mystery. The answer IS the mystery".

The king and his child rested in their relationship, acknowledging the Word carried upon the wind, "*Shamayim*".

MARY

Years passed, Mary grew and matured. The events of her life unfolded in and around her like a scroll being written, even as in the moment it was opened. Her mother had named her in honor of those great matriarchs of old: sages and prophetesses, some virgins, and others to be as queens or wives to the high priests according to Divine appointment bestowed on Asher's daughters. So, while she was honored and called by the title, "Mary", that name which had been given to her by the king, she held secretly in her heart.

There in the seat of her soul, Mary matured according to her named reality. She grew in understanding and wisdom, balancing her passions, desires and inclinations according to the will and knowledge of the king. This was the beginning of a mystic, sage, prophetess, scientist and philosopher, who we only know, simply, as "Mary".

Tradition tells us that she was born around three hundred years before Jesus, though there are rumors that she was born some two hundred years earlier. Others proclaimed she was the sister of Moses.

It is said that she had a long life, filled with adventure. Mary met many famous people. Perhaps such reports were just imaginative tales. Perhaps she really did live and meet all these great men of history.

Whether the stories are true or not, we might find some pleasure as we imagine Mary sitting beside Alexander the Great, where she discovered the strategy and foresight of a king and warrior. We could envision her spending time in a laboratory with Aristotle, where she demonstrated (or learned) the ancient, Hebraic technique of pulling gold from water and returning it to its former state. Or perhaps we might entertain the possibility that she had discourse and debate with Philo of Alexandria concerning the role of women and the feminine energy of the creative process.

It is said that Mary dined with Peter. She saw Paul persecuting the brethren and then she saw him persecuted by the brethren. Perhaps she stood by the river watching Simon as he thought to ascend by his own power, but instead descended to the Otherside. Did she hold baby Jesus, his skin still kissed by the dew of the Divine?

Today, Mary the Hebrew is primarily known as one of the first alchemists. She was a spiritual chemist. Her writings are long-since gone, though she spent much time recording her thoughts, sharing the wonder of the spiritual reality she witnessed. Her words are said to have pointed toward the above by way of the shadows of physicality.

SECRET

Reflecting on herself as a child, Mary recalled a puzzling and life-changing question her king had once asked her. Taking up her pen to write, her shaky, elder hand etched into paper vibrations of wisdom. Her words pointed like a finger toward the speck of eternal gold that is mysteriously connected to the face of the king watching from above.

In her mind, she saw a glimmer of light, as an emanation of righteousness, moving in and upon the water of consciousness. Her lips silently moved, reverently formed the secret she and her king once shared. And then the soul that had descended into this world of action from above, breathed deeply, released and returned to the face who measures, records and names.

SPACE OF CREATION

The space of creation is as the expressed thought of God. It is held within God. This space is God himself. It holds within it a center. This center foundation is the space itself. It is equal to God. The center, like the space of creation, is as an extension of the Divine light of God. This is the Word.

If we could go into the center point of righteousness, we would discover that it appears like the space that holds him (God). He is a vessel of creation. Through him (Christ) all is created.

Within the Word, we would see an emanation (*Atzilut*) of the Word. That emanation is expressed as the fullness of possibility. This is the beginning of creation (*Beriah*).

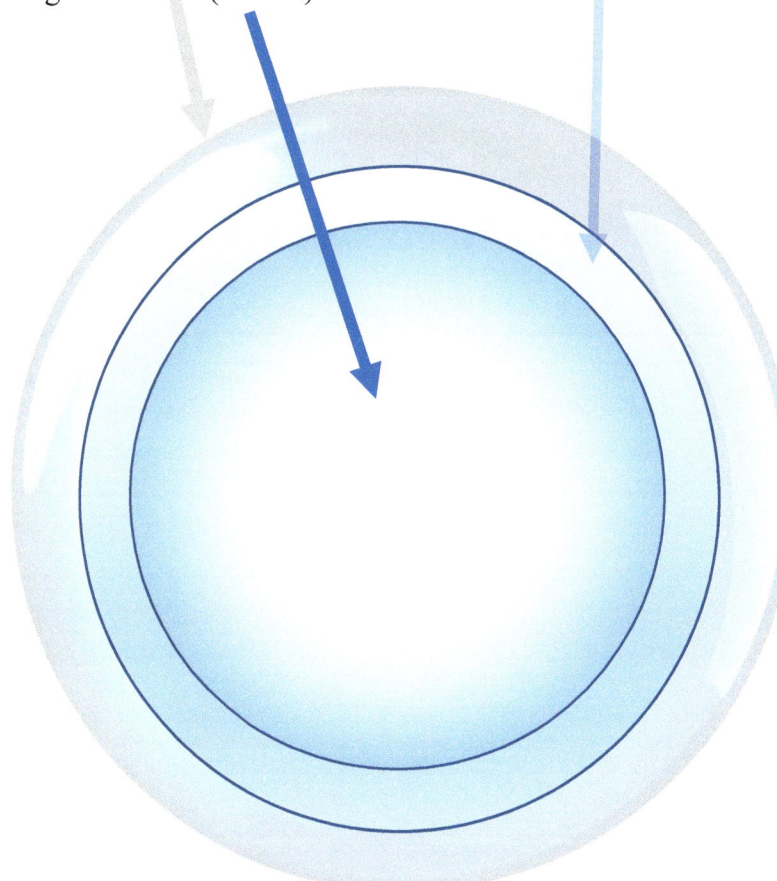

We have a circle with a point in the center. Within the point, positioned in the center of the space (house) of creation, is yet another sphere that holds within itself a point and within this point is yet another sphere of creation that holds within its center a space of creation. All of this is held within God, who is existence itself.

When we think of creation, as it occurred in the garden narrative of Scripture, we might picture Adam as a physical being or as a being of light. Then, in some manner, Adam left the garden. However, there is an ancient mystical view which forms the basis of spiritual science and what we call the Tree of Life model. Simply stated, God's first thought was his last action.

That first thought was of his Son. The Son holds within himself reflections of himself, so that all creation exists as a fractalization of the Son. The Son is the Word, who is the namer of creation. The Son is the Word, who is the potential of all that may exist. We could say that the Son is both the head of his body and his body, even though his body consists of expressions of himself.

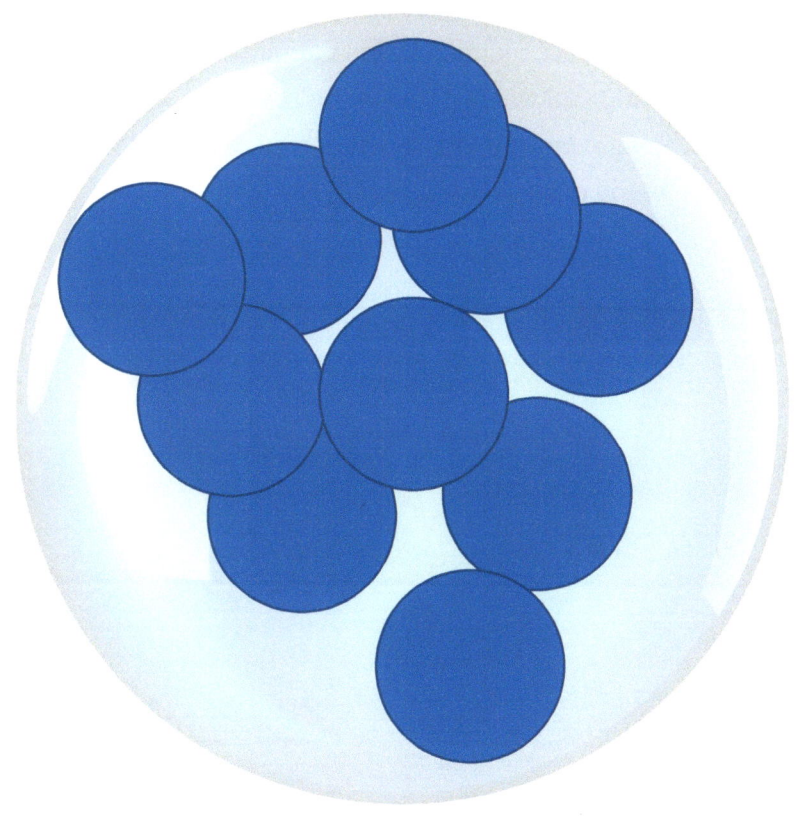

One way this has been described is as a comparison to Russian dolls, where each small doll is contained inside a slightly larger doll. We could also think of an onion, in which each layer is onion. However, each layer is held within and governed by its structure, which is the skin, the center and all that is within it.

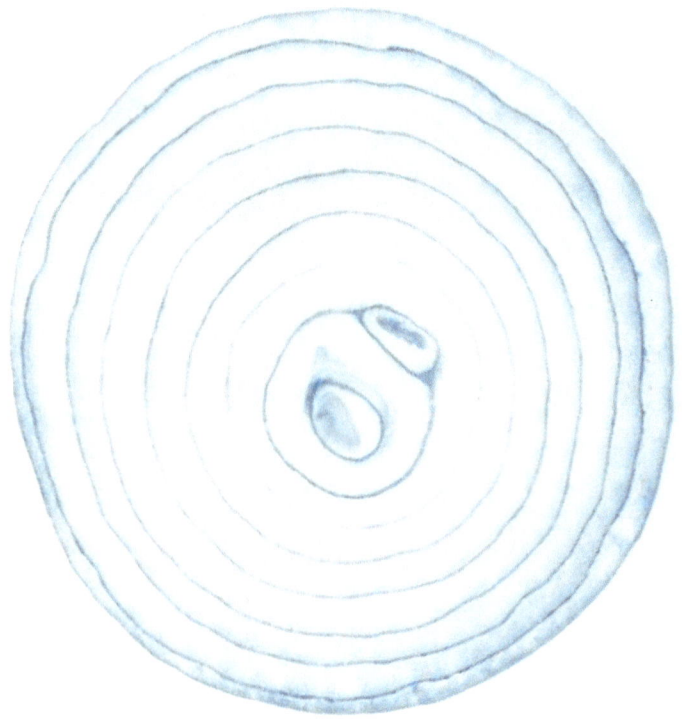

Or, we could relate it to a body of water, where each molecule of water is held, is sustained by, and moves within the pool.

Each layer of onion or each water molecule, may be unaware of the greater wholeness to which it belongs. If it is aware or becomes aware of the wholeness, it would be difficult for it to experientially know the wholeness of the pool of water or the onion in which it exists.

The next image symbolizes a small space of creation (man) that realizes himself as a vessel within an infinite space of creation held within God. As Mary the Hebrew might have said, this point (the vessel called man) who is simultaneously (existing in a state of) concealment and revelation, is as the first thought and the last action of God. He exists in an immediate, eternal moment that is outside of time and space. However, this vessel has place within God because all there really is, is God. Adam is the image of God.

This first thought of God is the holy light of God. He is the most holy temple who is referred to as the Son. He is uncreated. He is the full expression of God. He is the first and last Adam. He is Christ.

We could say this is you, or me, or even the entire body of Christ. Christ is within the individual and collective body. Christ is God's first thought (as his last action in an eternal now).

How can you say this?

Because Christ is the head and his body. Christ is within and amongst us – all. All of us, as one wholeness (One) are the emanation of God, held within Christ and sustained by him. Christ permeates all that exists. He is the source of our being. Indeed, he is all Soul.

> In that day you will know that I am in My Father, and you in Me, and I in you. (John 14:20)

> I have been crucified with Christ; and it is no longer I who live, but Christ lives in me; and the life which I now live in the flesh I live by faith in the Son of God, who loved me and gave Himself up for me. (Gal 2:20)

SONS OF GOD

For us, who live in time and space, we can only experience existing once we have our first thought. It is as though there is an awakening to consciousness. Breath flows into form, and in this movement, God's first thought (the Son, his Word) experiences "being" in physicality. You and I, as the body of Christ, are the emanation (*Atzilut*), the created (*Beriah*), the formed (*Yetzirah*), the lived out and experienced (*Asiyah*), expression of the Word.

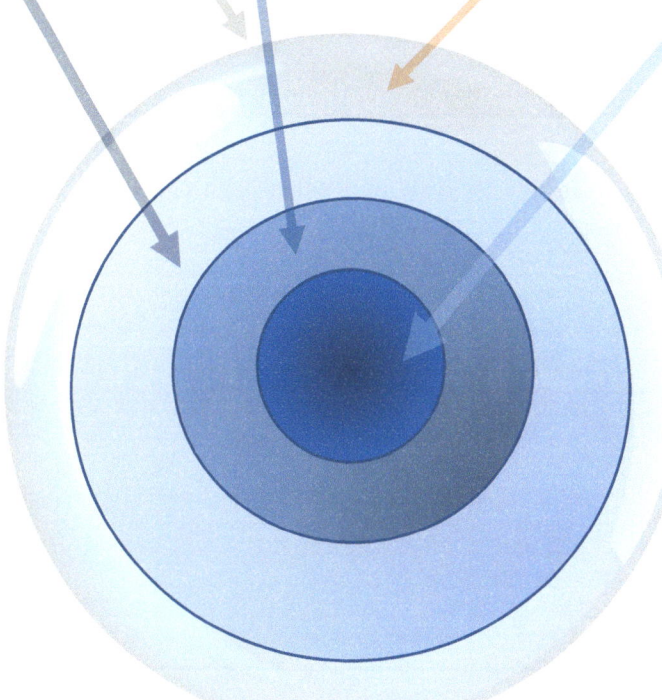

We are designated (predestined) to be mature Sons of God. Indeed, we have already been revealed in God's very first thought as his Son. Now (in our experience of time) we are revealed (within ourselves) as the Son. It is for this revealing that everything that is within us groans.

> For the earnest expectation of the creature waiteth for the manifestation of the Sons of God. For the creature was made subject to vanity, not willingly, but by reason of him who hath subjected the same in hope, Because the creature itself also shall be delivered from the bondage of corruption into the glorious liberty of the children of God. For we know that the whole creation groaneth and travaileth in pain together until now. (Rom. 8:19-22)
>
> I have said, Ye are gods; and all of you are children of the Most High. (Ps. 82:6)

The Sons, as sensory vehicles of God, experience being revealed as Sons. They, as one body, are revealed to themselves as being a Son, the light of God already seated in the above. They are the image and likeness of God.

The first thought of God (the Son) who exists in an eternal now, experiences and knows himself. Here, in this world of action (*Asiyah*), you and I, as the body of Christ, are revealing ourselves to ourselves (and all that is within us). We hold within ourselves (as the Body of Christ) all of who we are. We are the Living Temple of the Most High God.

MATURING SONS

Just as Mary (in the story) had an opening of her awareness to who she was, we may have enlightening experiences. This opening of the heart and mind to Christ is not usually a one-time event in which full revelation occurs. There is an ongoing process of maturation.

We dwell in a physical world where there is time and space. In this world, concealment might be equated to darkness and silence. We could think of concealment as darkness that hides something. For example, if someone is hiding a secret, they may try to cover it up or remain silent about it. They don't open their mouths and they don't reveal it to the light of day. As the Son matures, what was previously viewed as darkness is now perceived as it was. The Son discovers what the concealment is, its purpose and its plasmatic nature.

But, as beings of consciousness, who are expressions, emanations of God, we can glimpse the light that is within the darkness and hear the symphony beyond and within the silence. We can witness, record and name the contrast between light and dark, and discover the union of opposites.

EXPERIENTIAL KNOWING

We can experientially know ourselves, God and who we are in relation to God, ourselves and others. This experiential knowing often occurs in stillness. It is as though we leave the world, we're normally aware of existing in. Our conscious awareness of the world of action (*Asiyah*) dims. In meditation, contemplation or prayer, we leave it behind through stillness as we turn our gaze inward and upward toward God and the face, the image of God. That image is the Son. In silence and with eyes closed, in the darkness, so to speak, we can see the radiant light, and we can hear the symphony of the stars.

Now, of course, we can use the imagination to step beyond our normal, physical limitations. We can, by imagination move across time and space. We can recognize imagination as contrasted to what occurs in physicality. We are also able to recognize our different states of awareness. We can distinguish between a dream state and a state of prayer.

Imagination, dreams, prayers and visions of the night are known by us experientially, even as we can know the events of the day. We can measure our experiences. We record our experiences within ourselves. We can give them name. And, we can even name into existing a new idea, thought or experience, before we know it experientially or act upon it. We could call this, "creative imagination".

We might measure some object or measure an experience before we experience it. For example, we could measure our thoughts much like one might measure a building by way of a blueprint. This is the power of intellect, of understanding (*Binah*). We can classify and organize. We can discover new ways of communicating our ideas, experiences, senses and feelings.

The universe, which we hold within us, expands and contracts. With every experience, we grow and mature. We become as new expressions of who we are until, ultimately, we let it all go. Then, we return to who we really are; the face who measures, records and names.

However, it is possible, even while we live in the physical world, to experientially know and be who we really are. We are the image of God. We are the sensory vehicle of the Divine.

GOD

Christians identify with a triune God: Father, Son, and Holy Spirit. We can relate with God as three in one. However, even within the trinity, God is One.

Here oh Israel the Lord our God is one.

Christ is the Creator. He is uncreated.

God is not a man up in the sky with a big beard. He is formless. He is everything; but he is no thing. He is "nothing," in the sense that he is uncreated. He is no-thingness while simultaneously he is all there is. The name YHVH, is not God. YHVH is as a symbolic representation of God, by which we can have some form of relationship to he who is far beyond our understanding.

God exists outside of creation. However, everything is held within him. Somehow, he has allowed man to be the temple that carries him.

CONCEALING AND REVEALING

The first thought was concealed. The Rabbinic idea of this concealing is that God is concealed from man. God is not fully knowable by us. Before we are aware of him, we may not be aware of how he keeps us alive, and where we come from. But we may learn that there is a God.

We can discover this knowledge through the shadows of the physical creation.

When we experientially know that there is God, a desire grows in our heart to know him more and to be with him. According to the degree (intensity) of this desire, more of God's light comes into us. As the light comes into us, the greater our desire for that light expands. So, there is a kind of interaction with God where he reaches out to us without us knowing it. The more that we reach back to him, the more he responds to us.

If you go into a room filled with a very bright light, you won't be able to see everything in the room because the light is blinding. But, if a speck of darkness suddenly appeared, then you would realize, "Wow, there's something here!"

Similarly, light reveals and destroys the darkness. Anytime you bring light into a dark room, the darkness disappears. However, darkness points us toward the light. This is the idea regarding how the shadows of physical reality, even the shadows of evil or error, can point us toward righteousness and the light of God.

We are free to connect in relationship with ourselves, with God, with others and with God's dominion. We can rest in the stillness that we find in relationship with God. In this rest, we may have the opportunity to hear and to know God.

The Concealing is a forgetfulness.

Everything is concealed until there is the thought of it. God is ever present, even though we may be unaware of God.

As we have an ascending thought, it is as though we are carried into the above. From the above, we discover that thought expressed is as a holy lamp. The Word of God is the fullness of the light that shines from the Holy Lamp and is the Lamp.

To ascend above the concealment is to be within the Mind of the Lord. In that Mind, we find that we are the expression of God's first thought. We are God's last action.

Christ is the Word of God and is God. Though he is above all, he is in all and sustains all. By the thought of God expressed (Word) all was created and completed in him for his glory. The only reality is that God is One. All our experiences, actions and creations are held within he who is the sphere of existence. All potential for what exists is within him. He is the point that determines what exists. He is the single point to which all that exists returns.

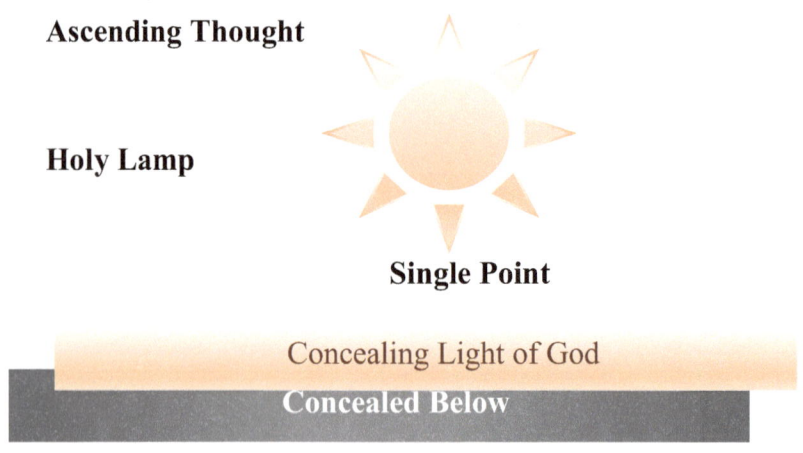

Ascending Thought

Holy Lamp

Single Point

Concealing Light of God

Concealed Below

In the beginning was the Word, and the Word was with God, and the Word was God. (John 1:1) "[a deep structure] emerging from thought ... called by no name ... Through this mystery the universe exists." (Zohar, Daniel Matt, Pritzker edition, 2004, Stanford University Press, Vol 1, p. 7-8, 1:2a)

Christ is the Word of God. He is the light of the Divine. He was (from the very beginning) with God. He was One with God. These concepts regarding Christ correspond to what is called, *"Ein Soph Aur"*.

Christ is above all that exists. However, Christ permeates all that exists.

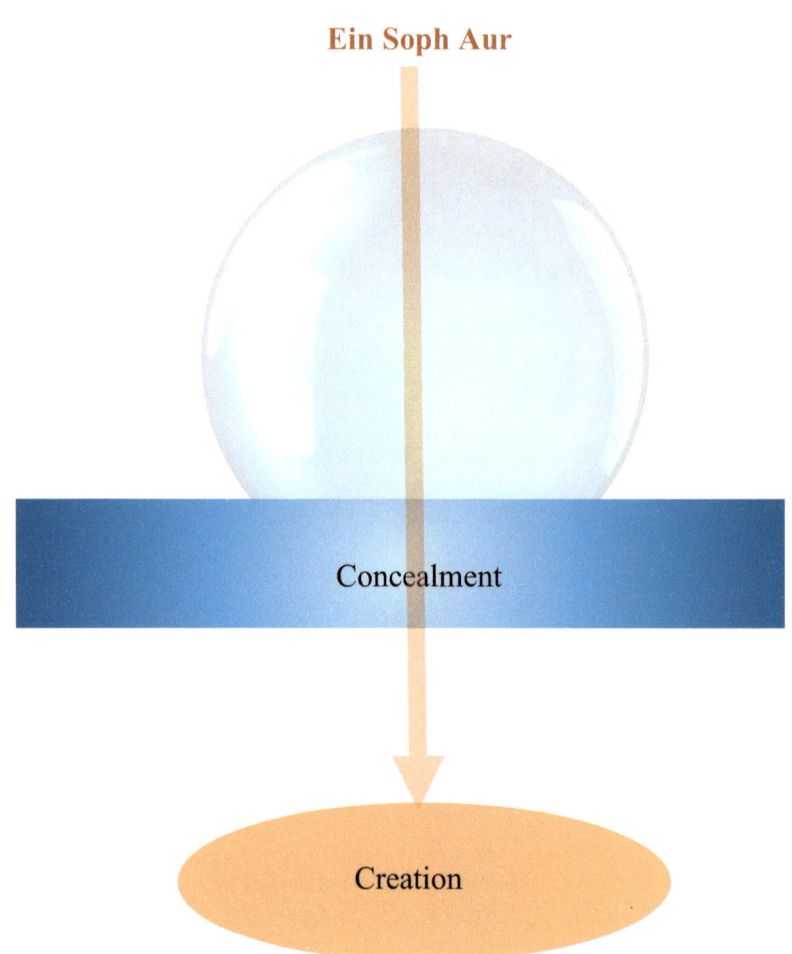

But we all, with unveiled face, beholding as in a mirror the glory of the Lord, are being transformed into the same image from glory to glory, just as by the Spirit of the Lord. (2 Cor. 3:18)

> God concealed a space within himself. This made room for the Light of creating to be "seen".

Christ is the space of creating. He is the Light of creating that fills that space. To Christ, everything is returned.

> He is before all things, and by him all things hold together. (Col. 1:17)

> Who is the image of the invisible God, the firstborn of every creature: (Col. 1:15)

Pure light cannot be seen if all there is in the space is light. To see the brilliance, the space needs darkness. Darkness points toward the light.

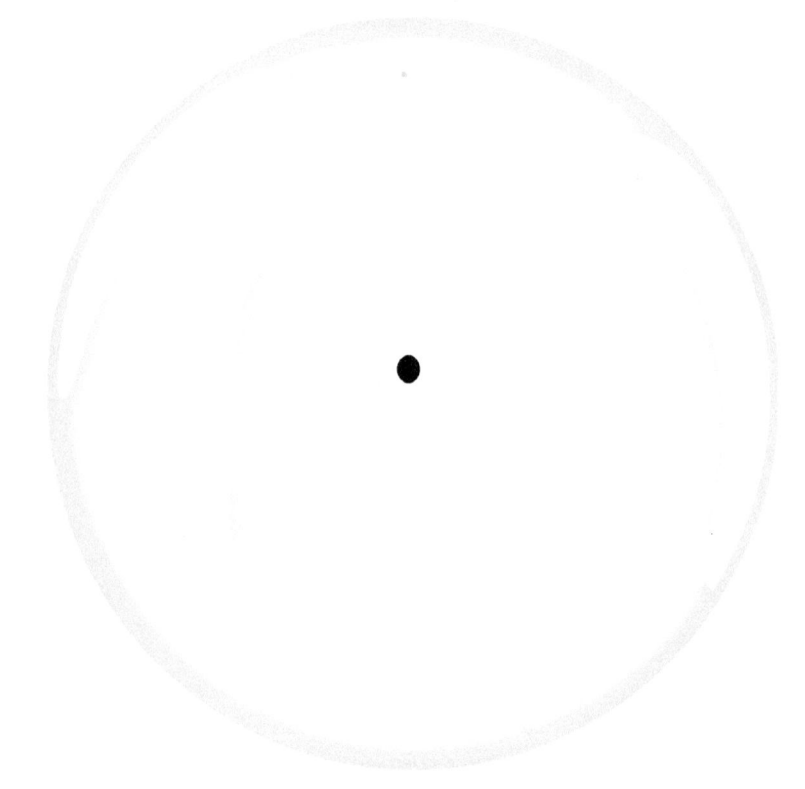

Divine light does not begin with a point. Divine light has no beginning. It is infinite. It is without position. It is all location. Divine light can only be "seen" when it is in a space of creating. The point of light "seen" is a revealing of Divine light. The point of light, in the space of creating, is a revealing of only some of the Divine light.

The point of Divine light is in the space of separation from the fullness of he who is Divine light. The point of Divine light is contained in the Divine light and is intimately connected to the Divine light, because it is the Divine light. However, it is concealed (dimmed, reduced, condensed) so that what exists in this light may to some degree comprehend and experientially know this Divine light.

RELATIONSHIP

What is relationship? Can we have a relationship with another person simply by looking at them?

God created us. We have a relationship to God. However, it may not necessarily be a right relationship. A right relationship involves communication.

We can be in the same room with other people. If we are looking away from each other, we may be aware that we're all in the same room. However, there is no energy put into the relationship. A man and a wife can be married for fifty years and never really have any energy moving on the arc of relationship between them.

It could be a matter of awareness, right? You can have a relationship without verbal communication. There are many ways that we can communicate. Can you think of different ways that we can communicate?

When two points are in relationship, a third point appears.

In relationship we have a choice. We can relate, then disconnect. We can send out a message or an invitation. We can receive a message or an invitation, or we can block an invitation to relate. We can unite in the relationship and strengthen it, or we can choose to weaken or end the relationship.

We can establish relationship so that even if we are across a room, across a nation, or on opposite sides of the world, we can still relate to each other. We can nurture relationship, lengthen, strengthen our connection through communication. And we can communicate in ways that need no words.

We decide what is acceptable and what is not acceptable in a relationship in any given moment. An Arc of Relating is a possibility of moving in relationship with each other. Relating is a choice. We are responsible for our own choices and for taking care of ourselves in relationship with others. We need to be clear about our boundaries in relationship. We can choose to establish an arc, move on the arc of relating, decide not to move any more on that arc and decide to break a relationship.

There are different ways of breaking the relationship. We can break it so that we're still aware of the presence of the arc of relating we once had. We may one day want to again act upon that arc. We can break the relationship saying, "I'm never going back to this again. It was in my past, and although it had some effect on me, I will never put energy on that relationship again". Or, we may try to ignore or forget the arc of relating altogether, and in certain circumstances it's possible to forget there ever was an arc of relating.

We've been created in the image and likeness of God. But, do we experience having likeness to God? Do we experientially know ourselves as the image of God?

> *Then God said, "Let Us make man in Our image, according to Our likeness; (Gen. 1:26)*

THIRD POINT

What is the third point that is formed whenever two points are in relationship?

There are different kinds of arcs of relationship. An arc of relationship does not automatically cause energy to move on the arc (in the relationship). However, whenever we put energy, desire and intention into the relationship, then we have a third point created. The new point is the result of a movement of energy. It can bring an object or the environment into the relationship. It can also extend an invitation to bring someone else into the relationship.

Relationship is an energy. Through movement, we bring into clarity what is not movement. We can recognize stillness by the experiential knowledge of movement. In a similar way, we can deepen our understanding of relationship by way of its absence.

We can sense the difference between different kinds of movements and different types of relationship.

It is possible to begin with a negative arc of relating and then shift the movement of relationship.

When we travel with God in a relationship based on similarity with him, everywhere we go we may find that we're seeing the situation, environment or others, from new perspectives. We begin to sense things differently because we go, not by ourselves, but united in purpose with God. We uphold, rectify and repair what has been broken within creation, that is, within his body, who is his creation. We participate with God in his ongoing creative process, rectifying, repairing, sustaining, integrating, and naming all that is held within us.

For two people to travel in the same direction, to have a unity of purpose, they need to face in the same direction. If you want to have a unity of purpose, so you're both working towards the same goal, it requires facing the same direction.

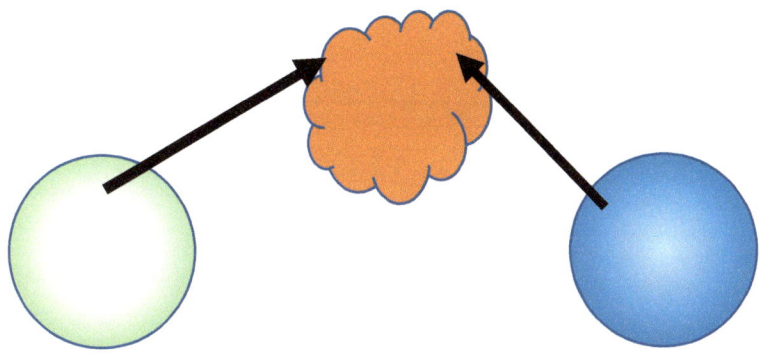

We could say that two people, having a shared purpose that entails moving in different directions, are in fact working toward the same goal. Though they are moving in opposing directions, they have a shared goal. Thus, they are facing the same direction (within themselves). The work may occur in the physical, intellectual, emotional or spiritual worlds; but they share the same goal within the arc of relationship.

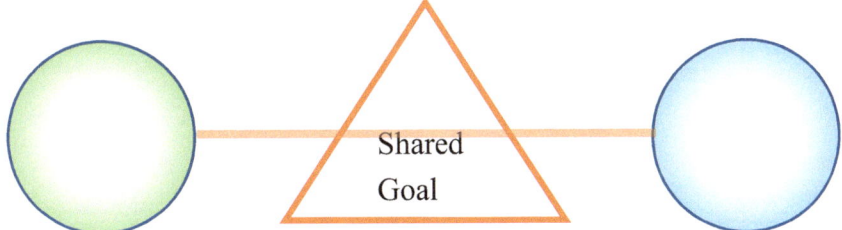

If we look at an arc of relationship, we discover that there are two different directions each sphere of influence may move in, while maintaining the arc. The point may be going in either direction. However, they are restricted to bi-directional movement because they are in relationship with one another.

As arcs of relating come into an agreement of purpose and extend outward, a grid of relationship is created.

MODEL

The Tree of Life (as it is drawn on paper) is only a model. It is a symbolic illustration. The Tree of Life serves as a map and compass. It is not the reality of our relationship with God, with ourselves, with each other or creation.

As we consider this model, if we're thinking geometrically, a point connected by a line can only move in two directions. If we have a triangular formation (involving three points) we then have more directions that the points may move, while maintaining their connections with one another.

In a grid of relationship, more potential within each point may be accessed.

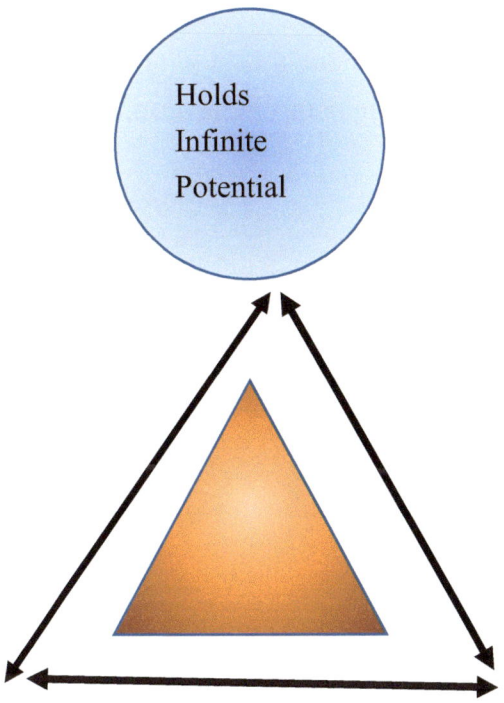

If we have a tetrahedral formation (a three-dimensional object) we not only have the directions that were present in the triangle, there are additional directions available. Each additional point connected to the grid allows more of the potential held within each point to be released and shared amongst all the points in the grid.

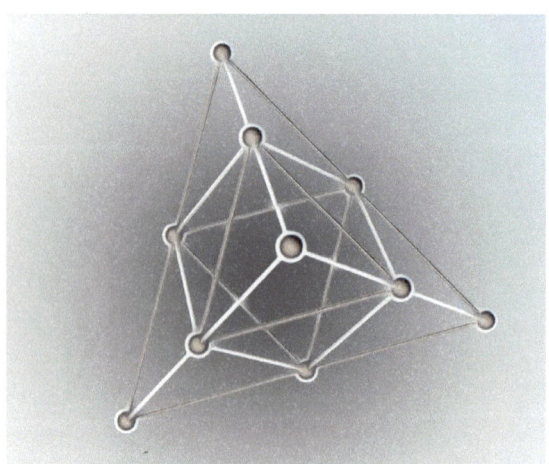

The tetrahedron is found in Genesis 1:1. Hebrew sages have referred to it as, "the weaving", or "the net", of creation. It is sometimes called the, "Shin", or the "fire."

This "great fire" is said to be source of all that may exist in creation. Everything is dependent upon this net of weaving. It is like a space of creating that holds and is all creative and experiential potential. Christians could liken this "fire" to Christ (the Word).

> Is not My word like fire, declares the LORD, and like a hammer that smashes a rock?" (Jer. 23:29)

That potential is the living Word of God. It is Christ.

> Now to him who is able to do far more abundantly than all that we ask or think, according to the power at work within us, (Eph 3:20)

MOVEMENT

Movement is the manifestation and realization of potential. Movement is an intrinsic nature of the structure of potential. Energetic points traveling on an arc is movement. An arc could be just sitting there, with nothing happening. When energy begins to move on the arc, it is said to be activated. We can activate an arc of relationship trough desire and intention.

We are in the sphere of creation. We all are held within God. We are a sphere of potential held within he who is the fullness of creation and potential. We (*as multiplicity*) are a (*unified multiplicity*) point and sphere (*house or temple*) held within the original One point/sphere (*God*).

We could think of a point as being somewhere outside of us. Maybe the point is perceived to be as a star in outer space. Or perhaps we might think of the point like a mountain or a palace that is located somewhere near to us. But when we experience the point (Christ) inside of us, we have access to it. We begin to grow into what God has created us to be. We begin to realize, not only the potential of who we are, but the responsibility this realization carries.

The experiential opening of the potential (held within us) begins within us, according to the movement of relationship with Christ (the potential).

INDEX

Adam, 6, 7, 8, 11, 12, 13, 14, 32, 37
Adam Harishon, 12, 13
Adam Kadmon, 8, 11, 13, 14
Arc, 55, 56, 58, 59, 60, 63
Archetype, 6, 8
Asiyah, 39, 41, 44
Atzilut, 31
Beriah, 31, 39
Binah, 44
Breath, 19, 39
Concealed, 9, 16, 17, 47, 48, 54
Concealment, 36, 43, 49
Consciousness, 5, 17, 29, 39, 43, 66
Creative Process, 28, 58
Darkness, 43, 44, 47, 53
Desire, 47, 58, 63
Dominions, 8
Ein Soph Aur, 50, 51
Emanation, 29, 31, 38, 39
Equivalence, 57
First Thought, 11, 32, 36, 37, 38, 39, 40, 41, 47, 49
Fractalizations, 17
Grid, 60, 62
Holy Lamp, 9, 49
Image And Likeness, 6, 41
Imaginal, 5, 21
Map And Compass, 5, 61
Measure, 10, 44
Midrash, 6
Mind Of The Lord, 49
Mirror, 24, 52

Moses, 27
Mystery, 26, 50
Namer, 15, 32
Otherside, 28
Peter, 28
Philo Of Alexandria, 6, 28
Point, 9, 10, 15, 17, 29, 31, 32, 36, 47, 49, 54, 55, 58, 60, 61, 62, 63
Primordial, 6, 8, 13, 14
Rabbi Akiva, 6
Rectifying, 58
Sabbath, 23
Sensory Vehicle, 41, 45
Separation, 19, 54
Shadows, 28, 47
Similarity, 57, 58
Space Of Creation, 15, 30, 32, 36, 52, 54, 62
Sphere, 11, 12, 13, 15, 16, 32, 49, 60, 63
Stars Of Influence, 24
Temple, 17, 37, 46, 63
Tetrahedral, 62
Thrones, 8
Time, 23, 28, 36, 39, 40, 42, 43, 44
Transformed, 52
Tree Of Life, 5, 6, 7, 32, 61, 64
Union Of Opposites, 43
Unity Of Purpose, 59, 61
Vessel, 7, 15, 17, 31, 36
Worlds, 5, 17, 59
Yetzirah, 39
Zohar, 7, 50

Recommended Books

[Divine Realm:](#) Who is God? Where is God located? What is our relationship to God? Who are the Sons of God? This Volume Introduces: Metatron, Sandalphon, Merkabah, Realms, Worlds, Dimensions, and the Prophetic State. Includes condensed information about the Tree of Life.

Belle Twigg is the author of many more books. To learn more, visit: www.academyonhigh.com

About the Author

Belle Twigg has a passion for right relationship with God through Jesus the Christ. She earned a BA, majoring in Transpersonal Psychology with a focus on alternative healing modalities and creative therapies, including those useful for dealing with PTSD, spiritual crisis, addictions, and for encouraging personal transformation. She then included an additional three semesters of study in Jewish and occult mystical practices. She has a master's degree in Consciousness Studies. She created a scientific mapping of alterations in consciousness through an in-depth study of Judeo-Christian Mystical States and general meditative states of awareness. Belle has been practicing and teaching ancient Judeo-Christian mystical practices for almost thirty years.

We would love to hear how this book has assisted you in your journey. Please leave a comment or review of this book

CPSIA information can be obtained
at www.ICGtesting.com
Printed in the USA
LVHW072009030420
652149LV00001B/3